RUNT

PATRICIA CORNELIUS in collaboration with
SUSIE DEE & **NICCI WILKS**

&

KEROSENE

BENJAMIN NICHOL

CURRENCY PRESS
The performing arts publisher

CURRENCY PLAYS

First published in 2022
by Currency Press Pty Ltd,
PO Box 2287, Strawberry Hills, NSW, 2012, Australia
enquiries@currency.com.au
www.currency.com.au

Copyright: *Less is More: The power of one in writing for women's solo performance* © Deirdre Osborne, 2022; *RUNT* © Patricia Cornelius, Susie Dee and Nicci Wilks, 2022; *kerosene* © Benjamin Nichol, 2022.

COPYING FOR EDUCATIONAL PURPOSES

The Australian *Copyright Act 1968* (Act) allows a maximum of one chapter or 10% of this book, whichever is the greater, to be copied by any educational institution for its educational purposes provided that that educational institution (or the body that administers it) has given a remuneration notice to Copyright Agency (CA) under the Act. For details of the CA licence for educational institutions contact CA, 11/66 Goulburn Street, Sydney, NSW, 2000; tel: within Australia 1800 066 844 toll free; outside Australia 61 2 9394 7600; email: info@copyright.com.au

COPYING FOR OTHER PURPOSES

Except as permitted under the Act, for example a fair dealing for the purposes of study, research, criticism or review, no part of this book may be reproduced, stored in a retrieval system, or transmitted in any form or by any means without prior written permission. All enquiries should be made to the publisher at the address above.

Any performance or public reading of *RUNT* or *kerosene* is forbidden unless a licence has been received from the authors or the authors' agents. The purchase of this book in no way gives the purchaser the right to perform the plays in public, whether by means of a staged production or a reading. All applications for public performance for *RUNT* should be addressed to Cameron's Management, Locked Bag 848, Surry Hills, NSW 2010; email info@cameronsmanagement.com.au; phone +61 2 9319 7199. All applications for public performance for *kerosene* should be addressed to Stacey Testro International, FSA # 68 Fox Studios Australia, Driver Avenue, Moore Park, NSW 1363; email syd@sti.com.au; phone +61 2 9358 4199.

Typeset by Brighton Gray for Currency Press.
Cover design by Alissa Dinallo.

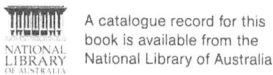
A catalogue record for this book is available from the National Library of Australia

Contents

'Less is More': The power of one in writing for women's solo performance
Deirdre Osborne   v

RUNT   1

kerosene   25

Currency Press acknowledges the Traditional Owners of the Country on which we live and work. We pay our respects to all Aboriginal and Torres Strait Islander Elders, past and present.

Nicci Wilks in the Dee & Cornelius & Wilks production of RUNT *at fortyfivedownstairs. (Photo: Pier Carthew)*

'Less is More':
The power of one in writing for women's solo performance

> How little do we know that which we are!
> How less what we may be!
>
> Lord Byron, *Don Juan* Canto XV, stanza 99

Imagine growing up with your needs unmet, your voice discredited or unheard, and never being able to form a lasting, mutually nurturing, emotional attachment with another person—except for once—and that ends in violence. How easy it is to stand on the judgemental perimeter of lives circumscribed by deprivation and damage and think, 'thank goodness my life is not like that', to believe that such people should feel shamed by their degrading, paltry existences.

However, what happens if those viewed as undeserving, social misfits do *not* internalise these projections of inferiority, but tenaciously assert their right to exist, stridently declare their wants, and take action to show the surrounding world—which tells them they are worthless, or negligible—who they are, and what they are capable of?

The plays paired in this volume confirm how theatre remains a provocative platform by which to confront uncomfortable moral questions. *RUNT* by foremost feminist playwright Patricia Cornelius in collaboration with Susie Dee and Nicci Wilks, and *kerosene* by newcomer Benjamin Nichol, offer searing explorations into those lives that are 'seen and not heard' in culture and society.[1] Premiering at two key Melbourne theatre venues, fortyfivedownstairs and Theatre Works

---

1 Of the many prestigious accolades throughout her career, leading playwright Patricia Cornelius (author of over 40 plays, including some co-authored, works for radio and screen, a collection of short stories and a novel) received the Patrick White Playwright's Award in 2006, the Patrick White Fellowship in 2012, and the Windham-Campbell Prize for Drama in 2019. She is winner of multiple Green Room awards and recipient of the award for Lifetime Achievement (2019). Ben Nichol's *kerosene* won the 39th Green Room Awards for Best Production and Best Direction and nominations in three other categories including Best New Writing in 2021.

respectively in 2021, these plays wilfully disturb complacent verities about class and opportunity to strip away the crassness of stereotype and open up intimate and moving portrayals in which 'every (under) dog will have its day'. We enter life's daily battlefield for those people (de)formed by the class, economic and gendered expectations which circumscribe citizens' lives, deeming who is valuable, who is disposable, and who is not recognised as possessing any viable social status at all.

Both plays had their geneses during the lockdown periods imposed by the Covid pandemic, a point in global history that presented unprecedented conditions and restrictions for negotiating life and art. The results, from Cornelius et al and Nichol, are creations of arresting, unapologetic, singular, female voices: Runt, 'a woman, small, shrivelled up' (*RUNT*, p.6) and Millie, 'Young. Fierce. Fragile. An unstoppable force' (*kerosene*, p.30). Housed within the compelling form that monodrama offers, of the smallest possible cast, these characters are conduits to representing experiences and perspectives seldom seen on stage. The letter cases of the plays' titles are noteworthy. The capitalisation of *RUNT*, redolent of shouting, asserts a strength from marginality, contrasting to the lowercase letters (associated with low self-esteem) employed for *kerosene*, which do not signal the enormity of the violence that follows. Both work take readers and audiences across an exacting and exhilarating dramatic arc, to deliver epics of the dispossessed, in which obsession and revenge, anger and shame, form a potent cocktail in contexts of unquenchable neediness.

At distinct stages of their career spectrum, Cornelius and Nichol both started out as actors. Cornelius's first writing, *Witch*, was a dramatic monologue she acted herself at La Mama Theatre. A graduate of the Victorian College of the Arts, Nichol was cast in a production of Cornelius's *Love* in 2019. His playwriting clearly owes a debt to his encounters with her unique dramatic signature, and is testimony to the considerable influence she has had upon contemporary Australian playwriting, a legacy which has remained underacknowledged in theatre historiography and mainstream programming. Cornelius has persistently galvanised the power of empathetic theatre through her distinctive capacity for extracting compassion from impossible subject-matter with often detestable characters. She routinely renders heroic the lives of socially dispossessed or morally compromised groups in plays such as *SHIT*, *Slut* and *Savages*, or those overlooked in their senescence like her profound, gerontocratic anthem, *Do Not Go Gently*. In reflecting upon the early days of the legendary Melbourne Workers' Theatre that she co-founded, Cornelius captures the central paradox of her aesthetics.

> How to write about and present a world that is tough, brutal at times, that is always about money, the lack of it […] about the loss of dreams, about anger, and yet make the work sing, make it hilarious at times, sometimes sublime? (Cornelius, 2022)

Nichol's commitment to social justice likewise informs his practice, including an early job with Fresh Theatre for Social Change and his own class consciousness, raised 'on the edge of Melbourne, the end of the train line. I never thought much of it until I went to university and I realised the suburb you grew up in impacted your understanding class-wise'. He notes, 'Of course, people can change and break cycles, but there's still so much of what you're shaped by in those formative years, which you carry on your shoulders—in the way you make decisions'. (Osborne 2022a) His observation captures one of the preoccupations shared by *RUNT* and *kerosene*, the causality between brutalisation and emotional deprivation—'Failure to thrive' (p. 7) as Runt presciently declares early on in her life's sorry cycle. Runt and Millie perfectly illustrate Bowlby's Attachment Theory. As newborns are biologically programmed to form an attachment to one main figure who is more important than all the rest, creating a primary bond—usually with the mother—serious adverse consequences result if this is disrupted, producing long-term cognitive, emotional and social difficulties. Runt, born last, is clearly the Darwinian dregs and—mantra-like—she knows it:

> Not a hug, a kiss, a single caress
> No loving me
> No loving me
> No loving me (p. 7)

Millie fares slightly better as father, siblings and grandparents rank next in Bowlby's hierarchy. 'I don't have a mum. Or a sister. Or an aunty. Or even a cool dad' (p. 32) Her attachment is pared down to 'All I got is Gramps' and an intense compensatory bond with Annie, 'Gramps and Annie' (p. 32).

In placing these two monodramas together, this volume opens up a dialogue about these very issues of nurture, *her*itage, legacy and survival and the ways in which class and gender remain a significant barometer of how creative contexts can sustain a social and cultural conscience.

The power of one

Monodrama (which has its origins in the dramatic monologue form) has been an important vehicle for aesthetically centring women's voices in contemporary Anglophone drama and performance, as have the artistic partnerships which have produced them. A brief trajectory in Australian theatre history includes notable late twentieth-century examples: Julie Forsyth and Jean-Pierre Mignon, in staging Alicia Tierney's *A Banquet of Vipers* at The Pram Factory (1981) and Raymond Cousse's *Kid's Stuff* at Anthill Theatre (1984), Wesley Enoch and Deborah Mailman creating *The Seven Stages of Grieving* (1995), Leah Purcell and Scott Rankin co-writing *Box the Pony* (1997), and more recently Declan Greene and Zahra Newman staging Kenneth Cook's *Wake in Fright* (2019) and Kip Williams and Eryn Jean Norvill adapting Oscar Wilde's *The Picture of Dorian Gray* (2022). Glennis Byron argues that the dramatic monologue uses 'issues of representation and communication' (p. 144) to create a persuasive conduit for (disingenuous and unintentional) revelation of character, as infused with dramatic irony. The monodrama performatively extends the dramatic monologue. If a dramatic monologue invites a reader to posit an audience, a monodrama assumes one. As the dramatic monologue does not necessarily aim for the reader to align themselves with the speaker, or even the auditor, the performer of the monodrama relies upon the audience member's alignment of identification with them. What *RUNT* and *kerosene* bring in performance (distinct from the 'safety' of reading them) is the challenge to not look away, but to be swept into the character's abjection and beyond, through the authority embodied in a solo woman performer.

Putting plays *together*

RUNT and *kerosene* both evolved out of a closely collaborative and organic process between writer/actor/director. Having worked in various combinations with each other previously, performer Nicci

Wilks, director Susie Dee and Cornelius continue their collaboration that brought all three together in the internationally acclaimed *SHIT*. Cornelius describes herself as 'old school' in working with and for the actors ('gorgeous editors'), excited by the discourse that emerges between the ways they 'say things with their bodies' and her writing. (Osborne, 2022b) A female triumvirate, the compositional relationship of Cornelius, Dee and Wilks is theatrically vivifying. A triangle or triad (unlike a dyad or dialogue) promises an unbroken conductor. It offers affinities, concord, discord and corroboration in various combinations and is always active.

Nichol's play evolved out of a short story, dramatically transformed with Izabella Yena in mind—his long-term collaborator. He notes of creating Millie, 'I knew the rhythms in which she spoke, the landscape she was going to live in and I knew what the climax was. I knew Izabella would be perfect.' As a male writer creating a female character, the drafting and redrafting was interactive with Yena, 'she would call me out on things that surprised her.' (Osborne 2022a).

kerosene

Nichol observes in an interview about another of his works, *Croydon*:

> I was curious to explore the long-term impact of what happens when we choose to totally dissociate from the pain of our surroundings, […] refuse to 'grow up' and take responsibility for our actions, and when we aren't equipped to care for the loved ones we feel obligated to look after. (Cybec Electric, 2021)

The comment resonates with Millie's fate in *kerosene*. Millie is a self-contained time bomb. In what proves to be ultimately unrequited love, the object of her lifelong devotion and attachment, Annie, tips into obsession—someone Millie would literally kill for. The play depicts how the intensity of the bond consumes Millie's life, contoured by an unspoken homoerotic love and impulses that simultaneously drive and impede her. As Nichol states, 'she can never quite catch up to what's happening around her because she's always looking over her shoulder at what was.' (Osborne 2022a) The play begins analeptically, then traces Millie's and Annie's schoolgirl oath of loyalty, sealed (in Millie's mind) when she gives Annie her family's opal heirloom. Nichol confirms he chose the very Australianness of the opal on purpose having 'been to Coober Pedy a few times' and that 'no stone looks the same, you can't tell if you have something valuable.' (Osborne 2022a) Such an observation underpins Millie's worldview, that she cannot interpret the complex contradictions life presents nor recognise what is precious. The palimpsest of *kerosene*'s origins as prose fiction is narratively evident. The playtext is shaped by economic, note-form language, connected in clusters of phrases that sweep us effortlessly between Millie's inner world and external actions. Employing numbered sections rather than scenes, '3' focalises *and* vocalises the disappointment she experiences at thirteen when Gramps gives her the opal. 'Oh. Shit. That's not fair. Oh. That's not fair. I can't hate it now. Oh. I look at him. This sad, soft old man. "Thank you. I love it. I love you."' (p.34) While Annie becomes a hairdresser, enters into a relationship with coercive-controlling Trent, Millie goes to university and travels abroad, but is unable to absorb any of the benefits of her experiences. They converge again in Millie's cataclysmic act of revenge upon Trent in a catharsis of violence. As with all aims and actions in Millie's life, her vengeance results in rejection—'She doesn't go back to him. But she doesn't come back to me.' (p.48).

RUNT

Metaphor is an intrinsic tool in Cornelius's writing portmanteau. In *Big Heart* (2017), 'generosity' is the means to unpick the multiple hypocrisies of international trans-racial adoption as colonial echo chamber. When Wilks approached Cornelius with the idea of herself as a runt around which to build a play, Cornelius made her a metaphor through the sack that hangs from a rope, to instantly evoke the discarded, abject, and rejected of this world. However, tracking Runt's adversity, is a constant projection of hope. In one episode, 'Love 1':

> I met a man and he likes me
> He likes me
> He likes me
> I like them small, he says
> […]
> My rabbit in a hat

> My tit for tat
> My little squeeze.
> My yes please
> Here here come sit on my knee (p.13)

The jocular repetition and anaphoras invoke a cockney rhyming slang, a nursery rhyme playfulness and delightfulness that then transforms to a prose poem form—tinged with menace, 'Look at the fists on him'. (p.14) In 'Love 2'—Cornelius confirms it was a late addition— (Osborne, 2022b) Runt, believing she is loved, allows herself to *feel* love. This exquisiteness is the high point—but also the tipping point. There is dread at turning the page. As anticipated, the markers of Runt's deprivation resurge by 'Love 3'. 'You're little but your appetite's huge. With wanting. The greed of you.' (p.15). She is blamed for lacking what she has never had, and the consequences are merciless. Put out by her mother, put in the bin by her teacher Mr Parsons, the huge man beats her up and deposits her out-of-doors, 'Like a cat. Just like that.' (p.16) We mourn her fate, even as Cornelius's mischievous dramatic-poetics create an oral/aural counterpoint to the thematic grimness.

Despite an earnest desire for collective politics, 'from the gut' as Cornelius puts it (Cathcart, 2021), Runt has had no training, no model, no mentor. She has only experienced the chasm between need and nourishment, wanting and not getting. She might 'have her day', freeing other downtrodden and dispossessed groups from the metaphorical sack of runtdom, but the task proves to be endless, impossible to complete. The episode, 'Born Free—a marvellous fantasy' where 'Runt sings and dances to her song of liberation' (p.19) portends a further plot twist. From being a liberator, her ego enlarges, spurred on by a lust for material acquisition, a lifestyle that signals significance and success. 'Leading the Dispossessed' a litany of reckoning and recognition, charts the trajectory from runtdom to status, naming pre-requisites that are logical, seductive and persuasive. Although Runt has the knowledge of how the system operates to crush people like her, simply freeing her fellow runts does not alter the conditions that breeds them in the first place. After achieving power, she loses sight of her origins, her runtness. In distancing herself from any connection to those subjugated, she begins to display a perfunctory disregard for their suffering,

> Time for all the unders, the missing bits, the undesirables, the untouchables and the deplorables. Too many of you, can't be looking after you. (p. 23)

and instead destroys them. But her elation—'I'm no fall between the cracks'—is short lived. Her hubris leads to her nemesis. She cannot escape from who she is. Alone and without any other option she voluntarily returns to her abject/reject state. It might seem a cruel curtailment of Runt's brief, audacious reprieve from insignificance, but the play's structure provides a scaffold in the life cycle of a runt, so that it is also the logical and practical completion of the action.

* * *

To not look away, but to face history that is ignored, sidelined or buried reveals how these plays might be perceived as part of a greater momentum edging towards what it means to face the colonial shame that seeps through the stitches of contemporary society's fabric(ation). Stan Grant writes, 'how confounding it can be to live as an indigenous person in a society—black society—now lacerated by class, gender, geography.' (p. 181) For Cornelius, the fight for equity, justice and decency is a collective endeavour centralising gender, but is foremost about class in a context where class and race are never openly talked about. She recently posed provocative questions about the place for her craft.

> Where are the plays that rattle, that rage, that disturb us utterly, that speak of our history and its lies, that show our diversity, that dare to reveal how despicable is this country of ours, that make demands, that are fierce and radical, going to find a home? (Cornelius, 2022)

Sara Ahmed argues, 'shame requires an identification with the other who, as witness, returns the subject to itself. The view of this other is the view that I have taken on in relation to myself; I see myself *as if I were* this other'. (p. 106) As Cameron Woodhead's review observes, '*RUNT* confronts you with transfixing dramatic art—the sort of play you watch, only to find it watching you right back.' (2021) Through her unflinching attention to such topics, and in her feminist politicised poetics that exposes misogyny and foregrounds class, Cornelius has been a prolific trailblazer. Yet, her body of work (arguably a canon), has been chronically neglected in Australian theatre seasons. In reviewing the premiere of *RUNT*, Anne-Marie Peard archly observes, Cornelius is 'a bit of a runt herself. Her career has been made in small theatres and independent productions'. One reason for this profile, Peard argues, is that, 'She writes about class and struggle and issues that are uncomfortable on our funded stages'. (2021)

What is most keenly apparent in both *RUNT* and *kerosene* is that they make us aware of how those people who do not have their emotional and physical needs met in their early lives, can too easily become casualties of worlds delimited by certain notions of success in citizenship and belonging—and in which they lack the capacity to participate. There are no conciliatory endings offered by either work, they refuse sentimentality. With uncompromising circularity, Runt emerges from, and returns to the sack. Millie remains fixed in needing evidence that she remains important to Annie through the symbol of the opal. Neither playwright offers comfort at the close of their plays but insist we sit with how and what it might be like to be so parched of the succour of self-worth.

Deirdre Osborne

My sincere gratitude to Patricia Cornelius and Ben Nichol for generous conversations about their work.

Deirdre Osborne PhD, Hon.FRSL, FRSA, Reader in English Literature and Drama, Goldsmiths University of London.

Works consulted

Ahmed, Sara. *The Cultural Politics of Emotion* [2004], 2nd ed. Edinburgh: University of Edinburgh Press, 2014.

Brindley, Michael. Review of *kerosene*, Jan. 2021. www.stagewhispers.com.au/reviews/kerosene

Byron, Glennis. *Dramatic Monologue*, London: Routledge, 2003.

Cathcart, Michael. 'Patricia Cornelius and Susie Dee Make Theatre for Runts'. *The Stage Show*, ABC Radio, Feb.22, 2021. www.abc.net.au/radionational/programs/the-stage-show/patricia-cornelius-susie-dee-runt-greg-fleet-bartok-bluebeard-oa/13178024

Cornelius, Patricia. Keynote Address, Australian Playwrights Festival, Apr.8, 2022. www.artshub.com.au/news/opinions-analysis/patricia-cornelius-on-urgency-and-risk-2542889/

Cybec Electric Meet Benjamin Nichol, Q&A. Feb. 16, 2021. www.mtc.com.au/discover-more/mtc-now/meet-benjamin-nichol/

Grant, Stan. *Talking to My Country* [2016], Sydney: HarperCollins*Publishers*, 2017.

Northover, Katie. 'Forget polite. Post-lockdown stages need grit, say theatre veterans'. *The Age*, Feb. 26, 2021. www.theage.com.au/culture/theatre/forget-polite-post-lockdown-stages-need-grit-say-theatre-veterans-20210218-p573sm.html

Osborne, Deirdre. Interview with Benjamin Nichol, Aug. 18, 2022a.

———. Conversation with Patricia Cornelius, Aug. 23, 2022b.

Peard, Anne-Marie. Review of *RUNT*, *Timeout*, Mar. 3, 2021. www.timeout.com/melbourne/theatre/runt

Woodhead, Cameron. Review of *RUNT*. *Sydney Morning Herald*, Mar. 1, 2021. www.smh.com.au/culture/theatre/fury-in-the-darkness-this-drama-confronts-our-cruelty-20210301-p576qp.html

Woods, Cat. '*kerosene* examines why people commit acts of violence', Jan.2, 2021. www.theage.com.au/culture/theatre/kerosene-examines-why-people-commit-acts-of-violence-20201231-p56r2e.html

RUNT

Patricia Cornelius in collaboration with
Nicci Wilks and Susie Dee

PATRICIA CORNELIUS is a founding member of Melbourne Workers Theatre. She's a playwright, novelist and film writer. She's the recipient of the Windham-Campbell Literature Prize and the 2019 Green Room award for Life Achievement. She's been awarded the Victorian, NSW and Queensland premier's prizes, the Patrick White Fellowship and Mona Brand Award for playwrighting as well as numerous AWGIE awards. She has written over 35 plays including: *RUNT*, *Shit*, *Big Heart*, *Savages*, *Do not go gentle...*, *Slut*, *Love* and *The Call*. Patricia's novel, *My Sister Jill* (Random House) was published in 2002. She's currently developing a feature film, *Stolen*, with director and co-writer Catriona McKenzie.

SUSIE DEE has worked extensively in the theatre as a performer, devisor and director in Australia and overseas for the past 35 years. She has devised many site-specific works and was artistic director of three companies: Melbourne Workers Theatre (MWT), Union House Theatre (UHT) and Institute Of Complex Entertainment (ICE) She has also directed works for MTC, Malthouse Theatre and many independent theatre companies and has been nominated for and won numerous awards. She directed Patricia Cornelius' plays, *SHIT* and *Love*, which both toured to the 2019 Venice Biennale Theatre Festival, followed by *Anthem*, a large-scale work that premiered at the Playhouse for the Melbourne Festival. *Anthem* then toured to Sydney and Perth Festivals. Her most recent collaboration with Patricia Cornelius and Nicci Wilks is *RUNT*, which premiered at fortyfivedownstairs last year and has just completed two more seasons in Brisbane and Sydney. Susie recently received the Australia Council Award for Theatre.

Kate Holmes

NICCI WILKS is a freelance artist continually creating and performing works of various art forms. She has been touring her work around the world for over 35 years, performing in 14 languages, from the Pitjantjatjara lands to 42nd St. NYC. Various companies Nicci has worked with include Circus Oz, Melbourne Theatre Company, Malthouse Theatre, KAGE, CIRCA, Melbourne Workers Theatre, Hothouse Theatre, Legs On The Wall, Company 2, Dislocate, The Flying Fruit Fly Circus and NORPA. Her one-woman intimate show *The Teensy Top* (she wears the venue!) has been presented at The Victorian Arts Centre, The Adelaide Festival Centre and at festivals around Australia. She directed the award-winning dark comic circus show *Party Ghost* and was assistant director and performer in the award-winning show *Taxi*. Nicci is a performer and co-creator of the highly acclaimed shows *The Long Pigs* and *Caravan*. She is a performer in the critically acclaimed stage production and feature film *SHIT* by Patricia Cornelius and was a co-creator and performer of the multi-award winning production *ANIMAL*. In 2021/22 she performed in *Fuck Fabulous Cabaret, THIS* for Rising Festival Melbourne 21, co-hosted the Adelaide Cabaret Festival, *Tale of Two Harpies* for Borderville Festival, *Fart Fabulous* for Rising Festival Melbourne 22, *The Teensy Top* for Adelaide Cabaret Festival 22 and co-created and performed her solo show *RUNT* in Melbourne for two seasons, at Brisbane's CIRCfest and at the Sydney Opera House.

RUNT was first produced by Dee & Cornelius & Wilks at fortyfivedownstairs, Melbourne, on 24 February 2021, with the following cast:

  RUNT   Nicci Wilks

Writer / Co-creator, Patricia Cornelius
Director / Co-creator, Susie Dee
Performer / Co-creator, Nicci Wilks
Composer, Kelly Ryall
Lighting Designer, Jenny Hector
Designer, Romanie Harper
Choreographer, Michelle Heaven
Stage and Production Manager, Bec Moore

CHARACTER

RUNT, a woman, small, shrivelled up.

CHARACTER

A sack hangs from a rope.

SACK ONE / FAILURE TO THRIVE

A sack hangs from a rope. It falls. An almighty thud resounds as it hits the floor.
The sack sits motionless in the middle of the space. Finally there's some movement—almost indiscernible. Gradually the movement becomes more frantic until, as if she has been birthed, RUNT bursts from the sack and spills onto the floor. She lays still for some time, taking great gulping breaths.

Can't suck
Can't suck
Can't get a hold
Can't latch on
No teat
Nothing to eat
No sweet creamy milk
Not a dribble
No suckle for me
Failure to thrive
What the fuck! How in hell am I going to survive?
Looking like a dead duck, a skinned rabbit, a scrawny chook
No sweet milk, no sweet breast, no sweet suckling, gentle snuffling, no warm skin to nestle in
No squeezing my cheeks, no chucks under my chin, no gooing and gaaing, no look at you, aren't you sweet
Not a hug, a kiss, a single caress
No loving me
No loving me
No loving me

She cries. Like a baby. She sits up and continues to sob. Occasionally she stops and listens. No-one comes. She looks around and then cries some more, her weeping slowly builds from snivelling, to sobbing, to bawling, to howling.

Finally, she stops weeping and stands—a rat cunning runt, eyes darting, alert to any sound. She stops suddenly and looks about. She snarls.

LITTER

RUNT *counts off her siblings.*

    Oldest. Basher. Set the tone, he did.
    Next. Hater. Oh, how she hated. Hated every one of us.
    A boy and a boy. Twins. Bashers.
    A girl. Non-descript.
    Another boy. Pig
    A girl and a girl. More twins
    Next one. Pretty. Curls. The best fed of all the girls.
    Boy. Basher.
    Boy. Hoarder. Never shared none. Not one crumb.
    Boy again. Basher.
    She stopped for a while. If she'd had me, I'd have been number thirteen. Should've been. Me and my twelve apostles, hee hee. But no, off she goes again.
    More twins. One talks and talks and the other never says a thing.
    Boy. Big one. Favourite son. Bash the living daylights out of everyone.
    Twins again. Attached. Shared a bowel which one of them lost when they got split.
    Boy, boy, boy, and you've got it, a boy. And you've got it, bashers.
    Then one you couldn't tell.
    Next one's got a lisp. Is she cute? Not a bit.
    Next a big-boned one. Mum split. Nasty that. Very nasty.
    Next one's pasty.
    Second last. Born with teeth.

        Pause.

    And then came me.

        Pause.

    Runt they called me.
    Runt of the litter.

That's me.
Runt.

TUGGING AT HER SKIRT

RUNT*'s on the run, desperate, trying to get her mother's attention.*

Tugging at her skirt
Tugging at her skirt
Tugging at her skirt
Pestering her
Asking too much of her
You're asking too much of me
Do you hear me?
Too much of me
Too fucking much
Tugging at her skirt
Tugging at her …
Grabs me by the arm
Way too hard she grabs
Nails dig in
To become lovely crescent scars
Mum Mum Mum
Hi hi hi
Wanting something
Wanting something
Wanting something desperately
Mum Mum Mum
Whatever it is escapes me
Takes off, is on the run
I'm tired she says
I've had a long day
A hard week
A tough as guts year
A shit-filled life
Tugging at her skirt
She's had enough of me
Gives me a shove and I fall

Enough she says
You're sucking me dry
Sucking the life out of me
Sucking her dry? That'll be the day.
Me who never got a suck at all, no way.
Tugging … at … her … skirt
Enough of you
Enough of you
Lifts me up and drops me out the door

    RUNT *whimpers. For some time, she whimpers.*

SACK TWO

RUNT *holds the sack pulled tight with a string. Quietly, intimately, she talks to it.*

You're a runt
What are you?
A runt
Puny
Undersize
Underdone
Undercooked
Under under under
More and more under
Stunted
You are
A miserable excuse
You are
A diminishment
Shrivelled up
A weeping sore
Blighted
You are
A dried-up dam
A desert with no oasis
A pond gone dry

A failed crop
A bucket of slop
Something sicked up
An aberration is what you are
The slimy ring around a bath
The stink from an arse
A piss in the pants
A shit on a rug

> *She listens in close to the sack.*

Why me? Is that what you ask?
Tiny
Scrunched up
All mouth
Sucking and sucking
Never going to fill you up
Runt!

> RUNT *lifts the sack and suddenly brings it down, hard on the floor.*

HEARING VOICES

Whispers fill the space—the runts of the world whisper their discontent. She listens but initially cannot find their source until she opens the sack and is almost knocked off her feet by the roar of those forsaken, the runts of the world, that escapes it. Quickly she closes up the sack and the roar is stifled. She opens it in short bursts and the roar screams from it.

She lifts the sack and brings it down.

Silence.

TUGGING AT HIS SHIRT

Tugging at his shirt
Tugging at his shirt
Tugging at his shirt
Wanting him
Desperately

Wanting him to listen to me
Listen Mr Parsons
But got nothing much to say
Hey hey hey
I go
Hey hey hey
Listen Mr Parsons
Listen Mr Parsons
But no words come my way
Tugging at his shirt
In class
Lots of us
Can't be heard
Hey hey hey
Listen Mr Parsons
Incessant
Incessant
On and on
Can't help myself
Mr Parsons, Mr Parsons
Angry now
Mr Parsons
Louder now
MR PARSONS
Tries to send me away
But I stay
See me, Mr Parsons
Louder still
HEY HEY HEY
I say
HEY HEY HEY
He puts me in the bin
With the tin lid
Puts me in
Covers me up
In the dark
Gone. Gone. Gone

THERE WAS A LITTLE GIRL

In the dark.

There was a little girl, very little, tiny in fact. She felt them slings and arrows. She felt them deeply. Terribly deeply. All feelings she was. She cried. And cried. Tears by the bucket loads. In misery. Never enough. For her the smallest of portions, the gristle off the chop, the crust of bread, the lick of a plate, the finger swiped for a taste is all she got.

Hungry for affection too. A cuddle, the smack of a kiss, a caress, a moment of sweetness, hungry for it, too hungry, wanting it too much. She takes a hand and puts it on top of her head. She takes a hand and puts it on top of her head. She takes a hand … She grabs the hand and gives it a squeeze, grabs it and sticks it between her knees, grabs it and holds it tight and not lets it go. She puts her lips on lips and feels the wet of it, she takes the tongue and lets it snake down her throat, opens her legs and wider to let the fingers prod and push and shove. Wanting something nice. A bit of alright. Wanting something warm, not this, this burn she gets. Wanting it to feel good. Feel … Good. All she gets is hurting. Hurt, her feelings are. Constantly snivelling at the pain of it. Feeling way too much.

LOVE 1

RUNT *'s over the moon in love.*

> I met a man and he likes me
> He likes me
> He likes me
> I like them small, he says
> He whizzes me around the dance floor, and I fly
> I can pick you up
> And throw you up …
> … and catch you
> Ooh, you're tiny, you're a little minx
> I could wear you around my neck
> You're my gold chain with a crucifix

Ooh, wee you are. A perfect size
I could put you in my mouth and suck you like a mint
I can tuck you under my arm
I can bundle you up and take you home
You're my pea in a pod
My rabbit in a hat
My tit for tat
My little squeeze.
My yes please
Here here come sit on my knee

> RUNT *stares up at her man.*

Here's a man, a big man, huge in fact and he's going to look after me, he'll make sure I've got everything I need. He'll protect me. Look at the fists on him. Look at the shoulders. The weight they can bear, he could pick me up and take me anywhere. The bulging muscles he's got. He's as strong as an ox. Never mind about his cock. Hee hee, I've got myself a real man, a good man, a loving man, a man who loves me.

LOVE 2

RUNT *walks a confident swagger.*

> Have a look at this.
>
> *She enjoys her new walk.*
>
> How can you resist?
> I walk, I talk, look, I take space.
> Who's me? I don't know me. Wouldn't recognise me if I fell over me in the street. Is that some tingling sprinkling dancing along my skin? Is that a smile I've got plastered across my face? What the fuck, is that me giggling?! Like a kid. Is that me speaking? Me? No, it can't be. Me sounding sweet. Me singing quietly. Me humming along to some tune I barely know. Listen to me. Who'dve believed it? Me not hungry. Feeling full. Not hungry! No way! Feeling pretty good, I dare to say. Feel his handprints, warm still, got a hold of me, got a good grip of me, not going to let me slip.

And I feel, yes I do, I feel some warmth, just a little, I let it flow free, here, inside of me.

RUNT *lets herself feel.*

LOVE 3

Surly, she growls a low growl.

You're wanting and wanting and wanting more.
Too much wanting. Wanting this and wanting that.
Drive me crazy with your wanting, wanting, wanting crap it seems to me.
Wanting to be happy, how am I responsible for that?
A hug. Tighter. A kiss. On the lips. You missed.
Say something nice, something sweet. Tell me I'm beautiful. Tell me I'm smart. Tell me I'm the best. Tell me you love me. Like you mean it. Like it's the truth. Tell me again, I didn't believe it. Tell me, tell me, tell me.
You've worn the love I had out.
You're little but your appetite's huge. With wanting. The greed of you. Never going to fill you up.
Runt.

ALL OVER

RUNT*'s eyes are shut tight, her body tense. She knows what's coming.*

Head's on the chopping block. On the plank about to be shoved off. Noose around my neck pulled tight. Waking to staring eyes in the middle of the night. Crushing my tiny hand in his great mit. His breath hot on the nape of my neck. Shoving me every chance he can get. Out of my way, out of my way, you're always under my feet, hanging around like a bitch on heat.
He picks me up and slams me against the wall.
Up and down, up and down, he's going for it, scratching my back against the bricks. He moves me around the room from the couch to the table to the floor. Takes me to the kitchen sink and shoves me under the tap, has me gasping like a drowned rat. I scurry out of his grip and

reach the door but he pulls me back by my foot. My elbows, my hips, and my nose, the very tip, scrape as he drags me across the floor. I'm a rag, a slip of a thing compared to him, huge, lumbering him.
There's nothing to you.
Yeah right. Nothing to me.
Nothing to you at all.
The thing he liked about me, that very thing, now repulses him.
No love left. All gone. Took off it did.
He takes a handful of hair at the back of my head and smashes my face into the floor. Hard. Wonder if I'm about to be dead.
He grabs me round the waist, throws me over his shoulder. I'm flopped and hanging over. And he's walking down the hall and out the front door. He puts me out. Like a cat. Just like that.

TOUGHEN UP

RUNT *strips down to her underwear—shedding of an old self.*
She takes up a position of balance and holds it for a long time.

Take up your hand and give yourself a smack. Like that. Yes, as hard as that. And now another. And another.
Hand over a candle flame, nails deep into your flesh, blade across your skin, bite into your top lip.
Toughen up.
Hold a cigarette against your skin, ten, fiteeen, twenty seconds, don't flinch. Build resilience.
It's a matter of discipline.
Plastic bag over your head, breathe in, breathe out, breathe in, knock yourself out. Tough. I am.
Boiling water, or iced, immerse yourself in. Endure it. Take it on the chin.
The toughest. I am.
Call me names. Anything you like. They bounce off me, like a drum, I'm skin tight. Can't get at me. Had it with tears. With whining. He did this, he did that, all that crap. Had it with pain.

Feel. Nothing. Nothing at all. Not one bit. Not a thing.

Be seen. Be loud. Fill the space. Not inconsequential you. Have weight. Always have something to say.

Harden up. Get tough. Don't be apologising because you're alive. I'm sorry, I'm sorry my heart's beating. Fuck that!

Take control, take it by the scruff of the neck. Hold on to it with all your might.

Be smart, smarter than the well-spokens, the big-talkers, the own-the-world walkers.

Retaliate. Eye for an eye, tooth for a tooth, wreak revenge, even the score, tit for tat, tit for tat.

SACK THREE: LIBERATION

RUNT *dons her clothes as if preparing for battle to the beat of a drum.*

It was an accident the first time. And then it became habitual, then it became an obsession I couldn't stop.

Hyper-alert, she listens intently. She opens the neck of the sack. A miserable whining comes from within. She looks about her furtively. Quickly she dips her hand in to drag something out by the scruff of the neck.

Count yourself lucky. Quick, fuck off.

She listens.

I heard their whimpers, I heard their gasps, heard them about to take their last.

She puts her hand back in the sack. And again, drags something out.

You too. Make a run for it.

She listens.

I heard their calls of misery: Help me, help me please, what have I done to deserve this?

Another dip in the sack.

So tiny, nearly missed you. Best of luck.

Some I got to just in time, a bit of mouth-to-mouth, a bit of a rub to the heart, sometimes a thump or two. Rebirthed some of them. Dead as doornails it seems and then along comes me. Some I missed, I admit, too far gone, couldn't get them back no matter how hard I tried.

She dips in again and again.

Sack after sack after sack. Thousands of sacks filled with miserable runts. In bathtubs, in troughs, in plastic buckets, in barrels, in freezers in the neatest of kitchens, in fishponds, a favourite spot.

Go! Go! Get! Take off!

Hanging from trees. Dragged behind cars. Some in basements, some starving in cages, some dumped in suitcases at the sides of roads.

In camps, in compounds, in shipping containers, on sinking boats, in holds of ships, on backs of trucks. Locked up, in prisons, in nuthouses, in institutions. Some left to rot on islands in far away places.

She dips in.

Here's your chance, make the best of it.

She empties the sack.

Go on. Get. Get. Get.

Hee hee. Who'd have thought? A vigilante. Me.

A CALL TO ARMS

> Got to get me a gun
> Going to get me one
> I know a bloke down the road, round the corner
> He'll have one
> Got to get me a gun
> It isn't right what's been done
> Got to fix it, got to put it right
> Going to make me some mess
> Oh yes yes yes
> Got to get me a gun
> Going to shoot someone

Going to go off bang,bang,bang
Going to scare the living daylights out of everyone
Armed to the hilt I'll be
Going to make myself known
Famous I'll be
Oh no they won't forget me
Going to get me a gun
Going to make me a bomb
Going to build me an army
An army, and then …
Going to blow this world up
Going to sing me amen

BORN FREE—A MARVELLOUS FANTASY

RUNT *sings and dances to her song of liberation, 'Born Free' by Matt Munro.*

LEADING THE DISPOSSESSED

>Not chosen
>Passed over
>No leg in the door
>No opportunities
>Kept poor
>Kept little
>Horribly small
>We've come to the end of it
>We say, no more
>Not considered
>Not cared for
>Pariahs, we're called
>Loafers
>Bludgers
>Thought stupid
>Ugly
>Worthless

We say, no more
Change is what we're marching for
'We want our rights and we don't care how
We want a revolution now'
Time now
Way time
For our share
Our bit
Our take
We want the dreams, the imaginings, the high expectations, we want them big
The good tucker
The oysters, shucked, with lemon or vinegar or something that helps them slide down quick
The champagne, to hear it pop and fizz up over the top
Lines of the pure white stuff to sniff up
Why not?
We want the Dolce Cabanas, the Yves St Laurents, the Ooh la las
The houses, the pools, the wine in the cellars, the scent of frangipanis
We want what you've got
The diction, the articulation, the walk, the tilt of the chin
Might take us some time but don't worry we'll catch on
We want the seats in the train or the bus, no, fuck that, in limousines, in cars worth a hundred thousand bucks
The seats of power too, on company boards, on committees, behind huge desks, in courthouses, in parliament
We're the johnny-come-latelies
About to give you a shove, to take your keys, to hack your bank accounts
Move over or we'll take the lot
'We want our rights and we don't care how'
We want …
We want …
Something else
We want …
Something bigger
Something … It's just beyond my grasp

The world to be better somehow
A life to be a decent life
We want ...
A change, a big one, huge in fact, a never go back
Something to give, to shift
Look at us
We're mighty
Look at us
We're strong
Look at us
We'll take you on
Runts of the world
We're here to stay
Runts of the world
We'll have our day
We'll take what is our right
Runts of the world unite

    RUNT *raises her head to hear a roar of approval.*

THE SWELLING

I've got some feeling again. It's a bit unnerving. It's not like feelings I've felt before. It's a strange thing that's happening to me, that's for sure. Me, Runt, is getting tall. No longer small, I'm growing, I'm swelling. I predict that the rate I'm going I might reach eight foot maybe or more. A giant I'll become. A magnificent one. Not a runt anymore

Not sure what got it started. Pride maybe? A bit of a novelty that. A bit of pride might've made me grow, I don't know. Even though I begged them to stop, the adoration might have nourished me, actually quite a lot. The respect I got, could've made me expand, swell from the pleasure of it.

Greatness. Extraordinary. Greatness. Astounding. Greatness ... trouble is, greatness forgets runtness.

SACK FOUR

RUNT *heaves a heavy sack across the floor.*

Sack after sack after sack after sack. Some so heavy they fuck my back.

The runts of the world too heavy a load. Too great a weight, a drain, a strain on the world. It's bulging, it's sinking, way too many of you.

RUNT *is still. She is struck dumb with the knowledge of what she must do. She closes the neck of the sack—the end of the liberation.*

Time ladies and gentlemen, time to move along. The sick, the slow, the poor, the fat, the ugly and the needy. The thick, the deaf, the dumb, the off with the faeries, the loony.

Time to go my little ones.

She listens into the mouth of the sack. Sad whispers escape it.

I hear them whisper.

I understand some of them say, it's true, we're useless, in the way.

Hope it all works out for the best. Hope the decision doesn't cause you unrest.

Hee hee.

Terrible squealing.

Some are squealing madly, scratching and biting each other in a frenzy in some wild belief there's been a mistake and they might somehow escape.

They smell blood. Their own. They're in a terrible state.

Angry voices in protest escape the sack.

Would you listen to that?! You're a dirty traitorous rat who should be lined up and shot, bundled up and stabbed, thrown in a dungeon to rot. Where's your sense of solidarity? Hee hee. Solidarity? Oh dear, I forgot.

RUNT *'s drawn to the sack again. The sound of terror escapes it.*

Time for all the unders, the missing bits, the undesirables, the untouchables and the deplorables. Too many of you, can't be looking after you.

> *She tentatively listens once more. Silence. Then the slightest whisper.*

What's that? Why aren't I in the sack?
I'm no fall-between-the-cracks. In the sack? No way, not me.

> *She whispers into the sack and it echoes eerily.*

Precious few of us can last.

> *She attaches the sack to a rope and hoists it up.*

> *She lets the sack drop. An almighty resounding thud.* RUNT *is elated.*

A WASTE

A terrible silence.

RUNT *is terribly terribly alone.*

She becomes small again.

Too small, too shrivelled, too shrill, too ugly. Such a shame. Not noticed, not seen, not thought of. Unfed, untouched, not held, not kissed, shoved and kicked. Snarled at, get to the end, get to the end, the arse end. Wait, wait, you little fucker, no tucker, it's a waste. A waste. You're not worth wasting a crumb on.

> *She opens the bag and crawls in.*

THE END

kerosene

Benjamin Nichol

Marnya Rothe

BENJAMIN NICHOL (he/him) is an award-winning writer, actor, director and educator based in Naarm/Melbourne. He has had writing developed with the Melbourne Theatre Company, City of Melbourne, Darebin Arts Speakeasy, ATYP, fortyfivedownstairs, Fresh Theatre for Social Change and Theatre Works. In 2021, he was Chantilly Studio's Artist in Residence.

For his writing and directorial debut, *kerosene*, Benjamin received awards for Best Direction and Best Production at the 39th Green Room Awards. He has received additional nominations at the Green Room Awards for Best New Writing (Independent Theatre) and been shortlisted for the Rodney Seaborn and Max Afford Playwriting Awards.

As an actor Benjamin has worked both nationally and abroad, with performance highlights including a national tour of *A Midsummer Night's Dream*, and a European season at the Teatro Biennale in Venice of Patricia Cornelius' *LOVE*.

Benjamin holds a BFA (Acting) and a MFA (Writing) from the VCA.

Izabella Yena in the Theatre Works production of kerosene. *(Photo: Jack Dixon-Gunn)*

kerosene was first produced at Theatre Works, St Kilda, on 20 January 2021, with the following cast:

    MILLIE   Izabella Yena

Writer / Co-director, Benjamin Nichol
Performer / Co-director, Izabella Yena
Producer, Jack Dixon-Gunn
Lighting Designer, Harrie Hogan
Sound Composer, Connor Ross

CHARACTER

MILLIE
    Young. Fierce. Fragile. An unstoppable force.
    Once she enters, she does not leave.

1.

Love is a funny thing. It's always there. Every smell. Every word. Every moment. You can't choose it. Or change it. Sometimes for a moment, you forget it, or you think you do, but all it takes is a spark and it's back, burning like a bush fire. You're a prisoner. Tethered. Chained. Robbed of sleep. And freedom. And choice. Stuck in the same never-ending loop of could'ves and should'ves and almosts and maybes.

Beat.

But that's okay. Cos as long as it's there, as long there's hope, then you're not empty. You got a reason to wake up. To wash. To eat. To work. To sleep. To repeat. Love is a perfect stain that you never want to see fade.

Beat.

I'm not sorry about what I did. I'm sorry about a lot of things. But I'm not sorry about that.

2.

Swimming sports. Coloured flags line the fence. 'Lilydale Community Poo'. Someone has torn down the 'L'. Dumb.

Beat.

A baggy singlet and boardies hide my tummy and legs. Sunscreen in my eyes. Folds of flesh. Cystic acne. Patches of wiry prickly pubes. Chucked a tanty when they tried to make me swim laps. Not gonna admit I don't know how. Not gonna learn. Not getting wet. Not taking my top off. No-one's gonna make me.

Beat.

Bored. I shuffle. Itchy. Picking at something. Something wet. Huh. Something red. A patch. Only a fifty-cent coin, but still, a patch of red. Perfect centre of the Tigers' footy towel I told Gramps I hated but he bought anyway. A patch of red. Glaring. Screaming. Exploding. The only colour in the world.

Beat.

'Oh my god. Millie is on the rag.' I don't look behind me. I know they're staring. I know what they'll say. I can sense the whispers. 'Dirty bitch.' 'Grotty mole.' 'That fuggo Year Seven doesn't know how to use a tampon.'

I don't.

Beat.

I don't have a mum. Or a sister. Or an aunty. Or even a cool dad who knows how to talk shit and get down with the kids. All I got is Gramps.

Who is good. And fair. And warm. But old and awkward. Also probably gay, so defs not good with girly stuff. Also, Annie. Of course. Annie. Gramps and Annie. But Annie's not here. Probably kissing a boy by the canteen or scabbing a dart off a Year Eleven, and without Annie to explain, I don't really know what is happening to me. I mean I kinda do. Obviously. I suspect I know. But Annie has two older sisters and has almost had four boyfriends so she will definitely know. And even though I know I'm not, a part of me thinks that maybe I might be dying. Which is scary. But also a relief. Cos at least then I'd be free from this feeling. From the stain on this towel. From this deep-rooted sense of humiliation that will never ever ever ever ever leave me.

Beat.

I'm up. Sly. Subtle. Power walking. Just to leave. To get out. Passing the Year Tens. No shoes though. Hot concrete. Fuck. I stumble. Fall. Face plant. Fuck. Dropped my towel. Fuck. My towel. Someone picking it up. My towel. Trying to help. 'Are you alright?' Fuck. They'll see. They'll know. My shame. My shame. My shame.

Beat.

Don't know why I made the decision, or if it was a decision, or why I thought it would even make things better, but I'm up again, and running this time, not towards the exit, towards the diving pool. Running, straight at the water. I'm diving in, well, falling in. Thrashing and blubbering, still bleeding, I sink. The water turns red. Blood pouring out of me as my lungs fill with chlorine and my shame billows around me. Bubbles reach the surface, my throat is burning, filling with water, I'm sinking, down, down, down, down, to the bitter end. But then something tears at my hair. Rips it from my scalp. Wrenches me upwards. Up towards light and life. Air.

Beat.

The water isn't red. It's blue.

Beat.

Ahhh. My hair. Wrenched again. Dragged into the change rooms. Annie? Annie. Annie. She slaps me. Hard. 'No matter the consequence, no matter the cost, we got each other.' Then, hugs me. Tight. Not letting go. Turns on the tap. Strips me down and lets me wail. Hard and sloppy and ugly into her shoulder. 'I can't go back out there,' I say. 'Not ever.'

Annie smiles. Chucks me a pad. 'Millie babe, no-one will even remember this.'

Beat.

She turns, marching out of the change room, out in front of the rows of salty sweaty douchebags, witnesses to the single worst moment of my life. Mr James is giving a speech. But then he's not. Cos Annie's ripping the mic from his hand. Dropping her dacks, bending over, holding the mic between both cheeks and letting out one of the sharpest, brassiest farts I've ever heard in my life. Sounds like the opening two notes of 'The Last Post'. My jaw hits the floor and my heart triples in size.

She was right. No-one ever talked about my moment again.

Beat.

No matter the consequences, no matter the cost. We got each other.

3.

'Happy thirteenth birthday Millie.' Gramps is beaming. Handing me a giant polka-dot box. I just know I'm getting a Tamagotchi. Been hinting for months. And now it's mine. I know it. I know it. 'Go on open it, open it.' Tear ribbon. Rip wrapping paper. Toss the card. It's mine. It's mine. It's …

Beat.

An opal.

Beat.

Bigger than my tit. Strange and round and shiny. An opal. What?

Beat.

'Do you love it?' Gramps drags me to the mirror. Pulls tufts of hair behind my ears. Clasps a chain. 'Suits you, doesn't it?' He's wrong. He's so wrong. He's so fucking wrong. Why would he give me something so wrong? 'They come from muck, but wipe 'em up, give 'em a bit of a work, and they sparkle ... just like you Millie. Don't you ever take it off.'

Beat.

Is this old man having a stroke? I look at it. This stupid sparkly eyesore. Strange against my crop top and trackies. I look at Gramps, still beaming, oblivious, but sobbing? Gramps isn't normally a crier. He'll scream. Howl. Moan. Shout. Rage. But not like tears. Never tears. But right there, definitely something embarrassing and wet leaking from both of his eyes. What is going on? What does he see in me that I don't? Cos it's not there. I promise.

Beat.

'This is the most precious thing we own. Your great grandmother dug it up. She wasn't great with words but her giving this to me was the closest she got to showing love. Now you're a woman, it belongs to you.'

Beat.

Oh. Shit. That's not fair. Oh. That's not fair. I can't hate it now. Oh. I look at him. This sad, soft old man.

'Thank you. I love it. I love you.'

4.

Years happen. School doesn't get easy. My tits swell. My teeth grow crooked. I get suspended for piercing my nose. I chop off all my hair. I cry about it in the mirror. Some days it's just too much.

Beat.

Threw a chair across the classroom in oh-two. Didn't know what to do with a kid who chucks shit at her teachers ... so they did nothing. Slashed a tyre in oh-eight. Punched a wall when Dad tried to leave. Again. Said I had too much of my mother in me and wanted to go back and live at the beach house. Wrote Gramps a cheque, kissed me goodbye and off he went.

Beat.

Even kicked Annie once. Accident. She got in the way. And I was aiming for the table. She shouldn't've tried to stop me. It just comes over me. Like a mist. Cried for a week after.

Beat.

'Heard you got fingered by Jim Stints behind the lockers on Thursday.' Jason Vassilou and his posse of pimply fuckheads. Leering behind me. Jeering across the oval. 'Said it was like a yeti down there.'

Beat.

School doesn't get easy. But I get tough.

Beat.

My fist is full of hair. Not mine. Theirs. They don't see it coming. They never think a girl is going to fight back. My knuckles, bleeding as they split bone from skin. Smashing a face into bins, portable walls, the canteen bench. Blood and salt. My own graffiti tag. 'Millie was here. Don't you forget it.' I'm a fucking legend. King. God. Slamming down. Standing victorious. Then. I realise what I've done.

Beat.

No-one ever expects a girl to hit back, so they definitely don't know what to do after she does. Not even Annie. Who's looking at me. Her eyes. Big. Wet. Not looking at me like I'm hers. She grabs my wrist. Squeezing. Dragging me away from it all. She screams. Afraid. Confused. 'Rip that cunt to shreds. But with your words. Never your body.' 'What's the fucking difference?' I scream back. But I'm also afraid. Also confused. I've seen Annie gut guys like a fish with as little as some side-eye. Rips me to size too. Hits me

even. Slaps and pinches for as little as spilling her nail polish. How's that different? 'Never hit men. It don't work like that. You gotta be cleverer.'
I'm not clever. Never have been. I try. I try to try. I try to try to be clever. But it's just not in my blood.

Beat.

Her eyes. That look. It frightens me. Never want to see that look again.

Beat.

Fumbling. Reaching to my neck. The opal. 'I'm sorry.' Annie looks up. Gawking. 'I'm sorry. I mean it. I'm sorry. Please take it.' Beneath her perfectly threaded eyebrows, her eyes narrow. Annie knows jewellery.

'This is worth serious coin.' 'Nah. In Coober Pedy they're everywhere,' I say, proud, for some reason. 'But it's your family's.' 'That's why I'm giving it to you, you dumb mole.' Boom. That look in her eyes. It's gone. I can breathe. 'Babes, it's perfect. I'll never take it off.'

Beat.

Moment I walk in the door, Gramps spots bare skin on my neck. He looks at his feet and doesn't say a word. Doesn't cook me dinner. Doesn't ask me to sing the harmonies in *Porgy and Bess*. Doesn't even look at me for almost a week. And I know this should bother me … but it doesn't. I'm burning, brimming, flying high all week cos I done good and made Annie happy. Made her mine. Cos that's all that matters right? If Annie's happy, I'm happy.

5.

Gramps was born in Coober Pedy. Born to a single mum. Steel in her eyes and fire in her heart. Mildred 'Millie' Jones. The first female miner, or so she said. Would leave him alone for weeks while she went underground, coming back with pockets full of raw jagged stones, ready to be polished, cut, tamed, till they glistened and sparkled. That was Gramps's job. He lived there till he was thirty. Cared for her right till the end. Moment she croaked though, he was off like the Road Runner. Beep beep. Trail of dust behind and never looking back. Ready for his life to begin.

Beat.

Life can't have been easy for Gramps. Alone in a tin house on top of a hill. With a mum who drank like a man. Dressed like one. Fought like one. And a little a boy who liked to sing. And draw. And file his fingernails while watching Lauren Bacall films.

Beat.

'Let's visit one day.' 'Coober Pedy is a cruel place for cruel people,' Gramps would snap. 'Then why'd you stay?' 'That's what you do for family. You gotta compromise. Love can be that glimmer of sunshine that pulls you through.' 'Even when they're cruel?' 'Especially when they're cruel. That's love.'

6.

We like to dance. Annie and me. Private concerts. Just for us. She touches my hips. Helps me loosen. Directs me. Guides me. 'Drop lower.' Whips my hair. 'Pop it. Shake it.'

Beat.

In grade six Miss Roper catches us and tells us it's degrading to women to move like 'that'. What? Happy? Confident? 'Like skanks,' she says.

Well. There's a reason she's still a miss. Besides. It's not skanky. Not sexy. Not yet. We're too young for that. But like ... foxy. It's foxy.

Beat.

Whenever our song comes on, we lock eyes, we jump in, and nothing can stop us. Not even at formal. The only one I ever went to. And I didn't even want to. I didn't. Our song comes on and without thinking Annie drags me in front of everyone. Everyone. Doing the dance. Grinding low. Making public our private. Annie, moving like waves. Me, a plane falling from out of the sky. But she's proud to be seen with me. In front of all these people. Opal thumping against her chest. Her eyes on me. Yeah. It's nice. I think I'm smiling.

7.

As a surprise to no-one, I don't have many boyfriends. Annie tells me I'll find my Chris Brown one day. I tell her Chris Brown is scum and that I don't care. It's not a lie. Boys don't like me and I don't like them. Not like Annie. It's like her sweat has a special spice that makes them come running. And she loves them all. Big. Small. Hairy. Old. Emos. Nerds. Footy lads. Even a couple from private schools. But never if they are shits to me. And lots are. Soon as I tell her that they've been ripping into 'lonely frigid Mills', then they're dropped faster than someone passing me a basketball in PE. They always think they'll win. But no-one beats me. Then she met Trent.

Beat.

Trent.

Beat.

Annie had left school and was hairdressing by then. She was real good. Great with colours. Could bleach you ice-white and not even burn your scalp. Trent was older. Lots older. Starting out in banking or … no. Something with money. Science. I dunno. I wasn't listening cos I didn't care, but he needed a trim and Annie was on shift. He was … well … sweet. A charmer. Could cut cheese with his jaw. And Annie really liked him. Like, really really liked him. So much that she started to change. She stopped making fart jokes. Or mooning the grannies on the bus. Or buying three double beef and bacon burgers from Maccas after school and stacking them on top of one another before chowing down. She liked him so much that she started to do what he said. Even when he said he didn't like her spending too much money, or going out at night, or wearing certain dresses, or working long hours, or working any hours, or seeing friends. Except me. She liked Trent, but she loved me. She had to. That was the rule. And I made sure he knew it. No matter the consequence, no matter the cost. I'd tell her he was a dick. When you love someone that's what you do. But she'd brush it off. Make it a joke.

'It's called compromise Millie. You wouldn't understand.'

Beat.

That's not my Annie. That's not my girl. Who listens to no-one. Who gives zero fucks. Who knows how to do everything right. Where's that girl? Where's she gone?

8.

Wrapped in his kimono, adjusting the needle of the record player, Gramps plays 'Don't Cry for Me Argentina' for the third time this afternoon. Happy Thursday.

Beat.

We sit, not really talking, not quite in silence. Him, in his big chintz armchair. Me, curled on the floor. He asks me how school was. 'Good.' Asks me if I want a snack. 'Nuh.' Asks me if I'm seeing Annie tonight … I turn on the telly and he stops asking questions.

Beat.

He never makes me study. Or makes me do chores. And for that I love him. I do. And whenever I ask for something, he does it. Anything. But he never kinda knows what I want. Or what to ask. Or how. Not that I know either, but I dunno, it'd be nice if he did. That's what families are meant to do. He just always seems to be sinking into that armchair. Reminiscing on the old times. Making another tequila sunrise. Drowning out Patti LuPone with his daggy operatic warble. Meanwhile I count down the seconds until dinner. Until *MasterChef*. Until bed.

9.

We're at a party. Me and Annie. And Trent. Hadn't seen Annie in weeks. Barely spoken. Longest gap we'd had. Even longer than when she did a central Australia camping trip with her stepdad cos at least then we spoke on the phone every day. But I don't care, cos half a box of wine deep and we're falling back into rhythm.

Beat.

When Trent ducks out, she cracks a joke about pussy discharge and lets out this deep aggressive cackle that knocks me off my chair. We're both sobbing with laughter, clutching each other. I'm bitching about Gramps. About how he's forgetting shit and getting grumpy. About how he's singing more and cooking less. I don't tell her that he fell in the shower. And that cos I was out, it was almost a whole day before anyone found him. I don't tell her that. But I do tell her that I graduated. Even did well too. 'Gonna go to uni. Don't know what I'll study yet. But with a mark like what I got I spose I have to right?' Annie agrees, 'I'd have gone if I had the smarts.'

Beat.

I tease her and squeeze her hand. I suggest we run away. Do one last trip before we become bitching career women. As a joke. It's only a joke. Unless ... She kisses me and smiles but doesn't meet my eye. She looks so grown up. Scarf round her neck. Just like a real lady.

Beat.

Trent's in the laundry and I decide we just gotta find a way to make this work. We all do. Make a 'compromise'. I pull him aside. Real calm. Give him a talking to. Just to make it clear that enough's enough and if he wants Annie he's going to have to learn to share. I'm sweet, make sure not to be too intense. He's sloshed and stumbling, nods along, and I think I've worked a miracle and finally gotten through until he reaches out and tries to stick his hand up my top.

Beat.

I tell Annie. Straight away. Obviously, I shove him, hard, then I march off and tell her. I tell her and she goes all white. I tell her and she thanks me. I tell her and they both leave. Together. No fighting. No screaming. They go in silence.

Beat.

Silence.

Beat.

And then a week later she texts me. Says they're moving. To Sunshine.

'Trent got a new job. Very exciting. Very last-minute.'
Sunshine's a long way from Lilydale.

Beat.

She texts me and says that she doesn't want me to visit. Texts me and says that I shouldn't reply. Texts me and says that she needs a break.

Beat.

A break from what?

Beat.

I drive straight over. They're already gone. The house is empty.

10.

I beg beg beg beg Gramps for a loan. Something to get me out. Away. A gap year. Gramps agrees. 'Sometimes it's okay to spoil yourself.' Through thick, camp calligraphy, he writes me a cheque. A gap month I decide after looking at the number.

Beat.

Never travelled before. But I'm ready. I think hard. Don't want to do Europe. Not like everyone else. Too busy. Too spenno. Gotta make the right choice. Has to be perfect. But that's too much pressure. There are too many options. I crack, I panic, finger on the globe, I point at random, I leave it to fate, and I end up in … Lebanon.

Beat.

Admittedly, an odd choice, but not a wrong choice.

Beat.

Everyone wants to talk to you when you're in a hostel. It's hot. And smelly. So much noise. I don't sleep my first two nights. And for some reason you're the rude one for just wanting to lie in your bunk. Fuck you. I'm not rude. Didn't spend an advance on Gramps's inheritance just to have sleazy Americans try and drunkenly molest me.

Beat.

All there really is to do is visit museums and memorials. Which I wouldn't do at home. So why would I do it here? Cars on the street nearly send me flying. I get lost more times than I count. I drink tap water. I get sick. For days. I look for my passport. Which I haven't lost. I haven't. Because it's in my bag. It is. It's in here. Somewhere. I'm not that stupid dumb tourist who fucks up on her first trip away. Fuck off. I'll find it.

Beat.

I don't find it.

Beat.

I visit the embassy. Need to cross the city to do it. Driving my taxi I meet a girl. Lydia. Her chat doesn't piss me off. We connect. Kind of. Her family runs a homestay and she invites me over. Won't take no for an answer. And believe me I try. Two nights I spend with them. Just two nights. But it blows my mind. Splits me open. Never seen life like that. Never felt it. Never lived it. Her family are so whole. Painting and cooking and proud of the world they've made. They're accommodating, but they don't seem to want anything, well, my money, I guess. But at least that's honest. At least I know where I stand. And right here, right now, I'm interesting. I mean so are they. But so am I.

Beat.

Lydia takes me on long drives and walks. I fall in love with markets. The noise. The smells. The silks. I fall in love with myself.

Beat.

Then the embassy calls and I fly home. Back. Same old city. Same old shit. I surprise myself and hug Gramps at the airport. He buckles, frail under my weight. We chat the whole bus ride home, well, I do. I don't stop.

11.

I'm so lucky. I am. I'm lucky. I am. I've got it good. I paint my bedroom. I join a gym. My muscles bulge, tight beneath my T-shirts. I'm so lucky. I get a job. Call centres. Just for a bit. For a year. Then, uni. Finally. Just like I said I would. Campus is huge. I get lost. I train as a dentist. I'm so lucky. I find a flat. My own. It's concrete and damp but as long as I pay rent it's mine. I'm so lucky. Gramps begs me not to go, wants me to wait a few more years. I tell him that the new me waits for no-one. He shakes and sobs. Says I owe him. Says he needs me. I smash a vase. He lets me go. To Sunshine. Annie's gone by then. Ballarat, I read on Facebook. Feels right though. To be close. Just in case. I'm so lucky.

12.

Fifty-hour weeks and I'm earning coin. Buy some hoodies. Nice ones. Buy a telly. Buy some plants. At first they die, but then they don't. The air smells cleaner when you got a plant.

Beat.

Gramps calls. Leaves me a message. I'll call him back. When I get the time, I'll call him back.

Beat.

New armchair. Due today. Want me to sign for it so I've taken the day off. Fucking Aus Post. I'm fucking stoked though. Sick of camping chairs like when I was a kiddie. This is my home. So, I bought an armchair from Kmart. Not on sale or nothing. Part of the new spring line.

Beat.

Gonna make this a home. Gonna drink my tea on that chair. Have a nap on the chair. Might get a cat. I'll watch telly on the chair. Watch *Survivor*. Watch *CSI*. Watch *The Bachelor*. It's silly, so dumb, it's gross, but fuck I love it. Nights turn into morning when *The Bachelor*'s playing. Stupid people doing stupid things but ending up happy. I know it's all fake. But fake isn't the worst thing in the world. Fake is okay if it makes you happy. Especially when you're sitting in your new armchair.

13.

I message her from time to time. She doesn't reply. Not even left on read. Just not seen. I think about her inbox. That number in the corner getting bigger and bigger. All those messages that one day

she'll click on and suck her back into the life she knew before. Her real life.
> *Beat.*

And it doesn't hurt me. Cos on Facebook she's tagged in photos. At the beach. At a wedding. Dancing at a club. And in all of them, after all this time, she's wearing my opal.

14.

Gramps dies. Found him on the toilet. Not me. A neighbour.
> *Beat.*

I drop out of uni. Teeth smell. Kids bite. I think about vet school. But don't enrol. I think about Gramps.
> *Beat.*

Cleaning houses. A few times a week. Working hard. Making some sparkle. But every week the grime just comes back.
> *Beat.*

I think about Gramps.
> *Beat.*

Fifty-hour weeks and I'm living cheap. Living off tins and beans and rice. I'm earning coin but I'm saving. I read online that you can buy a house in Coober Pedy for thirty K. 'Coober Pedy. A cruel place for cruel people.' The place where I belong. I can do that. I can do thirty. I know how to save. House is underground but that don't bother me. Sounds cool. Sounds quiet. Would be happy mining opals. A job with purpose. Pays well too, finding some precious in the muck. It's in my blood after all. Melbourne is cold. The city is spenno and wanky and the suburbs are brutal and empty. Coober Pedy cops a bad rap. I think I'd be happy in Coober Pedy.

15.

No point being idle. No point wasting time. No point losing sleep. I work. Like a dog. A machine. Long hours. Long nights. I work hard. Soon as my head hits the pillow, I'm out like a light. And it feels good. Well … not good. But it feels right. Then one night I get home from work and she's there. Out the front of the flat.

Beat.

Hadn't seen her in years. Must've been years now. But it's her. I was sure I was tripping balls. An angel. Sitting on my doorstep. Fallen from heaven but looking like hell. She has to lean against the door to stand. Hair's missing from one side of her head. Weepy wet wounds cover the side of her cheek and neck and breasts. Holds out her arms and falls into me. Can't look at me. Can't speak. I'm in shock. I knew Trent was fucked, I knew he was scum, I knew he shoved her, and she's no Shirley Temple herself, but I dunno, it's different seeing it. Split my heart. I should've known. I could've protected her.

Beat.

I take her in. Run a bath. Lift her up. We get clean. Rub her feet. Wash her hair. Smooth, smooth camomile through tight peroxide curls. At first, she doesn't speak, so I do. I tell her about the years, about work, about the books I'm reading, about the awful dates I've been going on, about the sad old army vet who lives up the hall and shares a room with his mother, and I'm a selfish cunt fuck slag awful rotten shit tits waste of oxygen but I'm glad to have her here, in my bath, in my arms, wrapped in my towel, tucked in my bed. And slowly she starts to mumble. To join in. She tells me about the disappointment of the Roos winning the grand finale. About Lindsay Lohan's guest spot on *The Masked Singer*. She's telling me she's thinking about going back to finish school and I'm smiling and I'm giggling. I'm fourteen again and so is she. But then she smiles, and I can see her front tooth is missing.

Beat.

Rubbing my thumb inside her ear, caressing every tiny baby bone, I whisper, real soft 'Beautiful baby, where is the bastard?' She looks at me, sad, like I've disappointed her. She says, 'Nah Millie, you can't darl. You can't. I just need a roof for a few days that's all. Just a few days till he calms down.' And I say, 'Babe he's tried to kill you.' And she says, 'Nah it's nothing like that.' I don't understand.

'Come spoon me,' she goes. 'Gimme a cuddle. Just like a sleepover.' She makes me promise that I'll cuddle her and do nothing else. And I do. It doesn't feel right but I love her guts and I do what she says. Friends do that. We listen. We compromise. Even if it has been a lifetime.

Beat.

And then morning comes. And I still gotta work, cos funnily enough the world keeps turning when shit hits the fan. I let her lie in. Leave a mug of Tetley next to her for when she wakes up. But the whole walk in I'm thinking. Thinking about that burn on her skull where all that beautiful hair used to be. Hair she made a living out of. Hair we used to braid when we was kids. But also, her smile. That big gorgeous toothy smile. And I must've been distracted, stuck in my head, plus I'm rolling a durrie, so I don't see it, this truck coming, zooming round the bend, nearly hits me, I'm quick and jump back, but the driver is this fat bald cockhead and I s'pose he got a bit of a scare because he yells out at me, 'Watch where you're going you dumb skank.'

Beat.

I'm blind. I'm transported. I lose all balance and breath. I choke a bit and I got to gasp for air. All I can see is Annie. All white and glowing and clean and it's like her beautiful face when we was girls but also that broken lost face I'd found in my driveway too. And she's dancing. We both are. Together. Not sexy. But foxy. Annie. My Annie. My beautiful girl.

Beat.

I can see again. It's clear and sharp and I don't reckon I've ever seen so right in my whole life. I know what's what. A gorilla has gone loose in my brain. Who is that cunting fuck to ruin my baby's face? Fuck Trent. Fuck him. Fuck him. Fuck him. Fuck him. Fuck men. I run, and I'm proper sprinting, haven't sprinted since I was small, but I'm running. I'm home. Wheezing. Going through Annie's phone. Scrolling though messages. Sending a text. Texts. Waiting. Waiting. Waiting. A reply. An address. Fuck he's dumb. Out the door. At a servo. Grab one of them big things of oil for your car. I'm running. Like a bulldog. That's me. A bulldog with a gorilla in her brain. I'm at his house. Oil in hand, keys in the other, threaded between my knuckles. Don't remember how I got in. Suppose I knocked? That's a pisser, imagine that? Walking up that pebbly path and knocking all polite. But then he's there. In the doorway. Staring. Confused. This cunt doesn't remember me. This cunt doesn't remember me. Cops a key to the gut. 'Fucking slag.' Then a boot to the head. And I'm in his house. Making it wet. Making him wet. Wet with my love, wet with my rage, wet with kerosene. Up the hallway, over the blinds, across the couches, down his throat. 'Remember me now you fuck?' He's writhing. Weak. Gasping. And I'm staring. Not blinking. Not breaking. Flick my lighter, trying to think of something clever to say, a real Double-Oh-Seven sort of thing, but nah, fuck it, I just want to see the bastard burn. I drop the light. Up he goes. Hot. White. Like my heart.

Beat.

I get home and chuck the bottle of oil on the kitchen table. It's pretty funny now I think that I carried it all the way home. It's pretty funny now I think that I bought a proper premium bottle, one for them real flash cars.

But I'm earning coin and I'm saving, and I reckon sometimes it's okay to spoil yourself.

Beat.

Annie is still in bed. Her cuppa's gone cold so I pour it out and make her a fresh one. I crawl into bed next to her and give her this real gentle kiss on the shoulder. 'No matter the consequence, no matter the cost. I got you girl. Forever.'

16.

Silence.

I don't remember the next day … or the next week … or that there was screaming … or that I go to bed alone … just remember that way she looked at me. That look in her eyes, the one I never wanted to see again … it came back.

Beat.

Houses don't burn as quick as you think. He survives. She takes the fall. Says it was her. Won't let me speak. Won't even thank me. Papers call her the 'bonfire banshee'. She doesn't go back to him. Even when he gets better. Learns to walk. To beg, like a dog. She doesn't go back to him. But she doesn't come back to me.

Beat.

Can't believe the way she looked at me.

Silence.

17.

I move. Again. This time it'll fix things. A slab of concrete, a slanty strip of tin and my pockets are thirty K lighter. The place where I belong.

Beat.

Fucking flies everywhere. So much space, and sun, and sand. Everything's red, flat, endless.

Beat.

Don't love what I see. But that don't mean I won't. We can learn to love. With time. With time, we can learn anything. I'm gonna be really happy here.

Beat.

Every morning, lady at the servo calls me darl. Burns my coffee. Makes chit-chat. Which I'm *learning* to love. Doesn't seem so bad.

Beat.

I'm gonna learn to weld. 'Bout time I did something useful. Trained my muscles. I been lazy. Getting flabby. I go walking. A lot. Every day. I walk. And walk. And walk and … haven't seen any opals. Not yet. Haven't really looked. Kinda thought they'd be everywhere. City girl showing her stripes I spose.

Beat.

I'm gonna be really happy here. I am. Because I got my glimmer. My thread to pull me through. My thing that keeps me putting one foot in front of the other. I got hope. I know one day I'll get home and she'll be there. Again. It could happen. It will. Cos on Instagram I see a photo. She's with a friend. In a pretty green dress. By a lake. And around her neck, hanging tight from a chain … she's wearing my opal.

THE END

www.currency.com.au

Visit Currency Press' website now to:

- Buy your books online
- Browse through our full list of titles, from plays to screenplays, books on theatre, film and music, and more
- Choose a play for your school or amateur performance group by cast size and gender
- Obtain information about performance rights
- Find out about theatre productions and other performing arts news across Australia
- For students, read our study guides
- For teachers, access syllabus and other relevant information
- Sign up for our email newsletter

The performing arts publisher

www.ingramcontent.com/pod-product-compliance
Lightning Source LLC
Chambersburg PA
CBHW042131160426
43198CB00022B/2977